bluebells in a jar

Noel Spence

A collection of Poems

Denise,
This is for the "wee room"
of your new house.
Best wishes
Noel Spence

AN OSWICA PUBLICATION

First Published 2006

ISBN 0-9548251-2-8

Copyright Noel Spence 2006

printed by The Universities Press (Belfast) Ltd

This book of poems is dedicated to the memory of my mother who, out of nothing, gave us everything . . .

CONTENTS

Introduction 1

THEN 5

BACK NUMBER 6

ELVIS 7

IN THE RED 7

THE EEL 8

FIRST BLOOD 9

MAGIC MUSHROOMS 10

PUBLIC ELEMENTARY SCHOOL 1950 11

SOUND EFFECT 12

SOUVENIR 13

SQUARE ONE 14

STREAM OF MEMORIES 15

APOLOGIA 16

NOW 17

A DEATH IN THE COUNTRY 18

AFTER THE THEFT 18

ARIEL 19

BAD BUSINESS 20

THE BROOD 20

CASTLEWELLAN FOREST PARK 21

CAT 21

CHRISTMAS 22

CAUSEWAY WALK 23

THE CHRISTMAS GROTTO BUILDER'S LAMENT 23

CRITICAL MOMENT 24

DROSOPHILA 24

DEATH OF A FROG 25

DIVIDING LINE 26

DOUBLE FAULT 26

DRUMKEERAGH FOREST AIR 27

EASY PICKINGS 27

ESCAPEE 28

FEBRUARY FRIEZE 28

THE EXECUTIVES 29

FIELD STUDY 30

FOLK CONCERT 31

GARDEN OF REMEMBRANCE 31

HEART HEARD 32

HOMECOMING 32

HEARTWORK 33

HIDE AND SEEK 34

INVITATION 34

HIGH RELIEF 35

HUNTER-GATHERER 35

HIGH SUMMER IN DOWN 36

JOINT ACCOUNT 36

INVERSE PROPORTION 37

IRRITATIONS 38

SCHEDULE 38

JOY KILL 39

PATIO STING 39

LIP SERVICE 40

NEW YEAR RESOLUTION 41

SAFEGUARD 41

NOT TOO BAD 42

PRACTICAL CRITICISM 43

PROPER NAMES 44

REJECTION 45

SNOWBOUND 45

ROBIN 46

SEASIDE CONFERENCE 46

ROCHESTER 47

SIC TRANSEUNT RES MUNDI 48

SIMPLICITY 49

UNDERCOVER CHRISTMAS 1972 49

STILL LIFE 50

THE THOUGHTLESS LOUD 51

WALTER COLOURS 52

WATERSHED 52

WEST END 53

WETLANDS 54

WINTER WALK 55

UP AND UNDER 56

UNFILLED FULL 57

NARROW WATER 58

THEN & NOW 59

CINEMA GOING 60

DIFFERENCES 61

FERRY LAND 62

MINDSET 62

ICONOCLASM 63

THE LAND BEYOND FIFTY 64

MOVING PICTURES 65

ROOFED IN 66

SMALL TOWN TRUMPET 67

GOLDEN OLDIES 68

THRESHING 68

THE WALL 70

FOUR WEDDINGS AND A FUNERAL 71

ROCHESTER WEDDING 72

THEIR MEETING MADE DECEMBER JUNE 72

ALLOTMENT 73

SWEET SURRENDER 74

ENDINGS 74

Introduction

"You should ask yourself before beginning any criticism: Does this writer have wisdom?" The place was a tutorial room in Queen's University, the time was the early sixties, the voice was Seamus Heaney's, and among his tutorial group were Noel Spence and myself, two Honours English undergraduates fortunate in their Tutor.

I have no doubt that the incipiently great man went on to elucidate and develop his simple critique: has a writer insight, perception, experience, sympathy; has he the art and technique to express these qualities; has he, in short, anything worth saying and the ability to say it, and will the reader be touched and changed by the experience? I expect our wise and soon to be famous Tutor went on to say all that and a great deal more, but if much that went in one attentive ear has long since gone out the other, this little nugget remains.

Even shorn of its elucidations, the shorthand critique still holds good, and its proviso must be met if a writer is to be taken seriously. Noel Spence's work meets the test; he has something to say and he knows how to say it. He has wisdom.

Brought up with his inseparable twin brother Roy in the County Down countryside, he had a toughly idyllic rural childhood where you were expected to work and get your hands dirty, where killing and skinning a rabbit was a commonplace activity.

Our bodies reeked of ivy, fern and whin, he remarks, in contrast to the city cousins with their *backstreet smell of oilslick hair and mildly fetid uncooked pastry skin.*

The difference, sharper in those days, between town and country is a recurring theme in these poems, and always with a sense of loss and regret.

While Noel Spence is not a poet who celebrates present or future issues, or deals with great events, but is unashamedly of the Ubi Sunt genre, his work is no sentimentalised or sanitised version of some lost ideal. There can indeed be lyrical glimpses:

and south, above a lichened grey stone wall

the brooding Mournes in misty blue

but the *red legged country children* in their poor *partitioned* (school) *room* were familiar with the smell of blood, *its sweet insistent terrible stink* as pigs were felled with *huge sledgehammer blows.* But set against the lyrical moments, the sometimes rueful humour and celebration of conventional rural realities, the poetry can assume a blacker, a positively frightening aspect. The rationale of *The Eel* (to my mind one of the finest poems in this anthology) I leave to the folklorist, but the verse now has a dark, mythic quality that evokes ancient legend and primal fears. Seen through the credulous eyes of an apprehensive child,

the eel,

the terrible timeless eel,

the lonely keeper of the well

has lurked there from time immemorial, for centuries, since

our granda's granda Quinn

was said to have put it there.

Legend is here tightly bound into the context of the personal, the nameable, the actuality of the child's own family, where the notion of 'centuries ago' and a real and remembered ancestor serve to validate the horror of the unseen monster, its infinite age and its infinite cold malice. This coupling of myth with the child's own identity and personal experience gives the poem its power and immediacy.

But the present supervenes, the *chromium tap* and plastic piping banish myth and terror much as Grendel's mother might be expected to fade in a setting of modern bathroom fittings. And with the loss of such frissons of childish fear, the poem tells us we also lose our childlike sense of awe and wonder.

It must have been early in that lost childhood of the nineteen fifties that the Spence twins discovered cinema. This was to become the abiding passion of both their lives, almost a way of life. Surely some of the eidetic qualities of Noel's poetry have their origins here: the telling glimpse, the shorthand of imagery, visual or verbal; the sharp economy of perception, the measured accuracy of narrative – all these borrow from the disciplines of cinema, its protocols and techniques.

Not only in cinema can we look for origins – the raw insistence of emergent rock music was to seize the twins in a lifelong passionate embrace.

one arose

on whom the new live world would turn,

a snarling, swaying elemental god

who'd spurn

the need to be articulate.

It is hard to resist this absolute enthusiasm for Elvis, the hillbilly cat of rock, and his compeers (a devotion by no means shared by the present writer), but the sheer gusto and joyous zest of the verse compels.

In retrospect, no time seems more remote than that postwar period of the Great American Dream, its boundless optimism and sense of promise. Noel Spence's poetry lovingly salutes the iconography of that Technicolor age, its throbbing jukeboxes and raucous glitz, the scowling rebellion of youth against complacent age. He characteristically laments the passing of not only the tangible artefacts of the period, but the loss of confidence and hope that underlies our more circumspect present.

A hankering for the past, for lost youth, a *nostalgie de la boue* are commonplace enough, but it is important that these poems should not be seen just as fainéant expressions of a generalised regret. The feelings that drive many of them are raw enough: pain, joy, bewilderment, but they have impelled him to anatomise and articulate them into the hard and demanding medium of poetry.

There is an intriguing parallel in another aspect of Noel Spence's life. His passion for cinema has already been mentioned – cinema, and <u>cinemas</u>:

> *What other buildings have a smell so sweet-*
> *stale carpet, warm dust, fusty cigarettes,*
> *Art Deco wall lights' dim red seashell glow;*
> *and oh the warm excitement in the gloom*
> *curved in a tip-up furry seat,*
> *secure in the dark red velvet womb.*

But in a bleaker time, the Picture House

> *that coloured vision*
> *suffusing dreams with love, adventure, war,*

was coldly sold out:

> *a planner's scalpel pen made swift incision*
> *and raised a bloodless supermarket scar.*

Far from just bewailing the loss, this articulate wordsmith and cineaste turned himself into an articulate and accomplished builder, carpenter, electrician and plumber to create a three dimensional work of art in bricks and mortar, a miniature replica of an archetypal Art Deco cinema with every detail lovingly correct.

The parallel is telling. Noel Spence sublimates feeling into action; he makes the films he wants to see, he builds the authentic cinema he wants to see them in – and he writes the poetry he wants to read.

3

I was privileged to see some of these poems a few years ago. Very much impressed, I urged Noel to publish them. I was surprised when, instead of his poetry, he brought out a first and then a second collection of short stories. I liked them and they were very well received, but I still believe that as a poet he is the better workman; his verse has more grip, more bite, a complete lack of cosiness, a more searching insight. The irrepressible humour has not gone, but the poetry is tougher, the images lodge in the memory, and the hardly definable quality of wisdom is more apparent.

He is in good company. Hardy, to my mind, was at his best as a poet, and I hope that Noel Spence, that gentle, reflective man of huge energy and douce melancholy, that unworldly dreamer and hard-headed pragmatist – a formidable embodiment of creative contradictions – will see to it that this Collection of poetry will be just the first, and that more will follow.

J.E. McKelvey   2006

THEN

BACK NUMBER

Those were the best days of your life
if only you had known…..
How often you have heard that said,
and something in your heart or head
that loves a time-zone called Instead
is always ready to agree,
no matter what the place or time.

With me it's like I'm on a phone,
a clear long distance recall line;
four pennies in, press button B,
I'm through to 1959,
and ciggy cards from Wills Woodbine.
We're watching Quatermass on BBC
and reading Famous Monsters Number 5,
blackberry birthmarks on our finger tips;
our small town has its silver screen,
(the midnight matinee features Jimmy Dean),
and shop where single cigarettes are sold;
a bedroom Dansette teaches how to jive,
the café jukebox gobbles threepenny bits,
its lit street warm with smell of fish and chips;
Robin Hood is Richard Greene,
True Romance is rife;
arched over all, in rainbow gold,
the red full glow of Marilyn's lips.

Yes, your exchange will purr a different tone,
connect you through
to a better number in another zone.
One thing's not new:
—— isn't it funny how
the best days of your life are never Now.

ELVIS

We shouldn't blame our teachers, I suppose;
they were only doing their job:
and yet it was from them we'd learn
the heresy of speech exactitude;
the arcane mysteries of verbs,
clause analysis, how to conjugate,
and dead archaic words
like preposition, parse, and predicate.
We listened in the passive mood....

Meanwhile outside of grammar one arose
on whom the new live world would turn,
a snarling, swaying elemental god
who'd spurn
the need to be articulate.
With scowling rebel eyes he chose
to writhe and pout and brood.
How fossilised were those
who thought his diction crude.
Our tailored tongues were strictly for the birds.

Would he have thrilled our soul
and made strange passions burn
had he been "all shaken up", or we been told,
"You aren't anything but a hound dog."

IN THE RED
To Heather

Red patent shoes she wore
that first night when we met
some twenty years ago, or more.
My mind's eye sees them yet,
though overdrawn from memory's store
and patently in debt.

For something warmed my soul,
like a flare of summer weather
will blaze upon a gleaming foal
and kindle purple heather.
We two glowed from the blushing coal
of shining patent leather.

THE EEL

Each time we dipped the bucket in,
breathless not to make a sound,
we knew the eel,
the terrible timeless eel,
watched unseen
from a slimy cave of bottomless hate,
the too small eyes
malevolent, cold,
the snaky length unwound.
Our granda's Granda Quinn
was said to have put it there
centuries ago, to keep the water clean.
We feared the malice of such age,
for none alive could tell
its slithering size,
from where
the eel had come, how old
the bleached-grey skin
that wrapped the lonely keeper of the well.

Down sunless, watery years it knew no friend,
no company of young, no mate,
its life a cruel concentrate
of silent, sinuous rage;
and we could hear
its noiseless presence, feel
a cunning without end;
mistrusted every shadowy crack
in its cell of dark moss green;
the half-sunk stick could be disguise,
those floating leaves a deadly hide.
A shudder rippled down the back
as the lipless mouth enclosed a heel....
The bucket filled with dry-mouthed fear.

The chromium tap and uncoiled alkathene
have long since killed off things that terrify.
The menace now is Interruption of Supply
in a white-coated world of fluoride.

FIRST BLOOD

Most folks, I'd say,
don't know the smell of blood;
it's not a thing they meet
in the run of a normal day.
I came early, too early, to its sweet
insistent, terrible stink,
an innocent at the slaughter.

In almost fifty years since then,
each time I've heard that tired phrase
a sickening thud
I close my eyes and think
I see once more those huge sledgehammer blows,
and hear the clamour of the scene –
pigs squealing in warm summer haze;
the crunch of shattered bone,
undeclamatory, dull;
the curses, grunts of sweating men;
black kettles pouring scalding water;
coarse hairy hides scraped barber clean;
flies buzzing in a dead pig's snout,
drip feeding from an oozing skull;
the ritual of the sacrifice –
white shaven bodies hung in rows,
hooked by hind feet, dribbling life
to the music of the sharpening stone,
soft throats, convenient bellies, neatly sliced.

Still   stronger than the loudest shout,
hotter than the scalding water,
brighter than the blazing blood,
sharper than the slicing knife,
deeper than the adult tongue can tell –

the knowledge of that gaping warm blood smell.

MAGIC MUSHROOMS

Don't touch the wicked mushrooms wild –
and overnight rose up a dark taboo,
a dread of clammy lardy things that grew
with whiff of blackwet peaty heath:
humped fungoid growths, corpse-white in the dew,
their leprous suet hide
frog-belly cold;
pale rubbery warts that smelt of mould,
their sickly stem a bloodless vein,
pernicious mink flesh wrinkled underneath
to poison horse or cow or child.
Day-brave we would footscatter wide
the misty morning sporous brood
and scent their taste of dank moist earth;
or whack with sticks the freckled putty brown
tough leather of their treeside pagan town.

It's said today that certain mushrooms would
affect the mind with weird hallucination.
For all our fear of plague and tumorous bane
we saw unveiled around their moonlit birth
strange lands that lie beyond this present place,
where sprites with rainbow radiance in their wings
flit down long golden lambs-tail lanes,
past flickering whitethorn fairy rings,
as pipes of Pan join in the pixie chase....
and we could safely feast on magic things,
inoculated by imagination.

PUBLIC ELEMENTARY SCHOOL 1950

Our teacher's slimly spouted pot
transfused a drip of hissing tea
that thawed through bottleneck ice-clot
and sewered the sluggish milk with cloudy mud.
Around the swollen belly of the stove
we gurgled through pale shivering straws
and felt the slushy fluid chill the blood.

Even then, on milkteeth minds, it wasn't lost –
the delicate china cup and silver spoon,
the fragrant hint of finer world perfume –
that raised her slender being high above
the humble poor partitioned room
and red-legged country chicken whom she made her cause.
That tall old-fashioned press was treasure trove
of folk-tales, eastern fables, story lessons taught
to hold us rapt like strange snakecharmer's tune,
and briefly break the bully grip of frost.

How did one single lady hold that crowd?
In face of muttering, boldness, raw stupidity,
she'd frown and scold, but never stoop to shout,
and shame upheld the rightness of her laws.
In stony ground she nurtured many a bud:
who can forget her warm triumphant fuss
when, first day there, my brother spelt out loud
the daunting letters twelve of *hippopotamus.*

No need today for grids of spellings on a page,
or learning heartless tables off by heart;
no inky jotters, pen nibs, blotters, errors rubbered out.
Perhaps the memory sweetens from afar,
but in a beeping, key-in, programmed age
where are the daisy chains, the artless art
of raggled bluebells in a jar?

SOUND EFFECT

You can remember them as well as I –
those endless radio Sunday afternoons
when lazy summer yawned and stretched out long,
her green smell fieldfresh in the hovering air;
one scamp cloud white in a matt blue sky;
a chirpy yellowhammer's chittering song,
velcro vagrant caterpillar in a Bo Peep box,
and Buddy Holly everywhere.

Respiring peppery lupin, creamy rose,
parental heads revived old wireless tunes
and family photos dated by the war:
a snapshot of a girl with fox fur stole
behind a high-wheeled swingboat pram;
a club of wavy cyclists in diamond pattern socks;
two sepia couples perched in Fair Isle pose
upon the running board of an Austin car;
a wooden teashop and laden telegraph pole
against a cliff of whitish Portrush rocks;
cobble-street shod shipyardmen beside a tram....

For us their world was cold, and yet,
behind dark glasses rimmed with crewcut sweat
we didn't see the power that warmed our earth;
as heat poured down, and bubbled tar
imprinted clothes stains butter couldn't shift;
as flameless match lit corktipped cigarette
and shimmering sunheat hazed the dry road wet,
we felt a heat that made the flat top lift,
but didn't know the source, raw rock 'n' roll,
though present at its loud volcanic birth.

SOUVENIR

That summer, quite by chance,
we parked our tubby Morris car
in a curved town on the coast,
its long street spiked with palms,
mountains vast against the sky,
warm doughnuts in the air,
cold sea-salt mackerel, clams.

We chose
not to move too far,
to see the town
on sauntering sandal feet,
enjoy the stir,
in raffia sunhat shade.

Before us, white and neat,
THE PALACE, One Week Only host
to horror, a thing *Half-Man, Half-Fly.*
A few shops farther down,
just past an upturned icecream cone
soft-soldered to the street,
THE CENTRAL BALLROOM, solid, square.
Its poster roared *Young Farmers' Ball.*
A smaller starred smart Him and Her
in starchy formal pose,
and challenged *Learn to Dance.*
The stipulated *Proper Clothes*
and altogether uppish tone
sidestepped the longcoat Teddy Boys
in Joyland's loud arcade;
they moved to thumping jukebox noise
and partnered one-armed bandits round the wall.
Near dodgem rowboats' tight expanse
we heard a tansad tantrum boy,
with new tin bucket, wooden spade,
bewailing lonely castles on the sand.
His freckled mum, with sundress, windmill toy,
perspired in a tearoom's prim retreat,
espresso cups on gingham red and white.
We watched poor pierrots rhyming on the strand,
and bought a 3-D viewer, Bakelite;
I have it still; the landscapes stand out clear:
a canyon, redwood pines, a waterfall.
These stereo pictures do not fade.
Outstanding too, kind memory's souvenir –
Newcastle scenes still seen, '58 the year.

SQUARE ONE

Beneath the snoring Tilley lamp,
the clothes damp on a pulley line,
and birdcage tarred with War Horse smoke,
we bandied button draughts across the board,
or breathed good luck on rattling eggcup dice;
climbed fast rungs near to sneaky ninety-nine
where, almost home, frail fortune finally broke
and, Adam-like, we paid the grievous price –
a graceless giddy downfall, serpentine.

Around the fire's expostulating sticks,
where cross-legged players squatted on the floor
like flickering Indians in a pow-wow camp,
we learned the segregation of Old Maid,
that handslaps beat the lawful call of SNAP,
that happy families grew in groups of four,
and wise it was that jokers were ignored.

Inside a room no bigger than a stamp
not only whist was played and won by tricks:
the yawning move might camouflage a trap,
and solid checkered ground could be a swamp.
As bread on forks was toasted, cocoa poured,
soft talk and hardbaked play would smoothly mix.

Behind the closed lid of the family door
the simple rules were read, agreed, obeyed.
In cottage warmth our playing caused no harm;
we couldn't know the life games yet to come,
where first man crowned won right to counter-tramp
upon opponents' heads, to press them under thumb,
and send them home where no love kept them warm.

STREAM OF MEMORIES

There's something tempting about a stream
and fundamental its appeal;
follow down its lazy twisting length
and feel
the urge to peer down, on your knees,
in places where the strength
of dark flow under checkered trees
invites a finger dip.

Elsewhere,
below a brambled overlip,
a dark and sullen pool would seem
to warn off all
but clouds of midges in the sleeping air.
Does that black stillness hide a slithery eel?

A little further on
the sheep have fed
and cropped the grass down to a tidy lawn.
Thoughts of campfires, tents and picnic ease,
and in your head
the making of a silver waterfall.
The muttering music now has led
to shallow waters where
an idle current combs the candy bed,
and hazels bend long shadows in the gleam.

Legs crisscrossed with briar scratches,
armed with jamjars, through the field
we broke our way to such a stream as this,
to catch the darting spricks.
Past years of sodden shoes and hasty patches,
whin jabs and thorn stabs roughly healed,
had taught us all the tricks:
raise the stone gently, let the fingers kiss
the quivering fish into the trap.
Then SNAP!
Scoop out. Is it a miss?
No, there's the flat mouth sucking at the glass,
and breast red as new bricks.

Our every impulse was to bring them home,
to keep them in a fishbowl clean and round;
yet sad experience had shown
they wouldn't last,
they'd float white-bellied, dead and upside down.

To have, to hold, to own
is love's dear tender show.
Far dearer are the memories of the past
when tender was the pain of letting go.

APOLOGIA

It didn't seem then
that we were doing wrong;
their deaths were just part of a game
for raw adventure seeking boys.

Hands poised with deadly care
and patient not to make a noise,
we stole in ragged shorts along
the lint-hole's reedy edge
to stone a gawky waterhen.
From red and yellow beak there oozed out mud
which in our innocence we took for blood.

Another of our hunting ploys,
to my eternal shame,
was standing on the bank above
to drop great boulders on the chicks,
those little black and bobbing balls of fluff.

And then there is the business of the hare:
with ageless cunning, in the hedge
we set the snare,
well camouflaged, precisely high enough.
The real surprise,
when, half-afraid, we saw the body there,
was not the weight and size
so much as the dark sad beauty of the eyes.
We skinned it, staining the slow brook,
the sleek fur now an archer's muff,
as studied in a comic book.

Among our other tricks
stands out the hazel rod we'd shove
down burrows, like a kind of wedge,
to scare out rabbits for our yapping cur;
the death squeal died upon the summer air,
the skin became a boy's own hunting glove.

Looking back, not wishing to escape the blame,
I recognise a truth that lies
behind the killing we were guilty of:
soft down, dark eyes, warm fur,
the death of beauty is an act of love.

NOW

A DEATH IN THE COUNTRY

They say his sister found him in the barn,
the one next to the hayshed's empty grin;
alone before he'd done himself no harm,
the limp boy with the spittle on his chin.

"He hasn't got a chance in life's hard game,"
his father said one day with bitter heart.
It's true that nature must share in the blame
to give an only son so poor a start.

The things that men will count on as of right,
like love and luck and always half a hope,
died in his pale blue eyes like failing light
while some dark knowledge noosed the neutral rope.

It's hard to see the sense in such a death,
or read a simple mind of fourteen years.
Perhaps the meaning in his strangled breath
hangs high above a sane man's civil tears.

AFTER THE THEFT
December '94

To try to trace a crime
back to its source
is to enter a snowshake ball;
nothing outlines clear at all,
mind blizzards blur the course.
Unsure of place and time,
unable to recall
the sequence of events,
and led by memory astray,
your progress is a crawl.
You try to force
a hopeless way
through whirling thoughtfalls dense.
Forgetful of the where's and who's,
blinded by If Only,
you lose,
in every sense,
and fall,
confused and lonely.

18

ARIEL

From this high point the white road wriggles far
to where, beyond a blue receding hill,
it sidles out of view,
in summer sun's smokedust.
On such a wishful, wistful day
the restless spirit can't but feel
importunate nudgings of the will
that urge an open road, the freeborn thrill
of soft surrender to the tyrant car,
and simply going somewhere far away.
The want becomes a need, the need a must.....
and oh the leathery rapture of the drive,
the sense that every rise hides ocean blue,
and life's best moments sit behind a wheel.

At some dim point, unmapped, unknown,
a gear is shifted down in mind's content.
The pleasure of the journey's overtaken
by fast compulsion to arrive,
and motoring joys seem somehow overblown.
Mixed in, like dark fumes in the languid air,
vague conscience over cares forsaken,
apostate thoughts of what's going on back there,
and shadowy half regret one ever went.

How can the human soul expect to roam
to gratify the traveller's need,
and simultaneously prefer
dissatisfaction felt at home,
unless, from body's destination freed,
it might indeed
be here, there, everywhere.

BAD BUSINESS

We did our bit. I mean
no one could fault us there.
(We're both still working every hour God sends)....
How we enjoyed her days at Kiddie Kare –
play times, plaits and plasticine;
then primary colours and kneesocks Persil clean,
and coaching – twenty quid an hour, I swear –
for College, the one the Higher Grade attends;
the riding school and all its pricey kit
and stabling of her birthday mare
that snickered with its well-heeled friends;
piano lessons, holidays abroad (time share),
a Gold Award presented by the Queen,
the Easy Payments Clio when she reached eighteen,
and flat in town (or glorified bedsit).....

Now look at how the sad bad business ends
and tell me if it's fair:
her life's whole happiness depends
upon some little lowlife shit
with studded lip and Rastafarian hair.

THE BROOD

One can't know everything,
and that's cold fact;
even so,
the lengths I go, the parts I act,
to dodge those simple words of truth –
I don't know.

Eyes thoughtful, brow intense,
I light a slow pipe, tap a tooth,
prevaricate, misconstrue,
use jargon terms that make no sense;
cause diversion, shake the head
(as if some things are better left unsaid),
feign deafness, cultivate a cough,
look absentminded, need the loo,
yawn, prattle, laugh the matter off,
or take a sudden interest in the view,

This smooth-haired litter, sired by *I don't know,*
crossbreeds with terrier-toothed *I told you so.*

CASTLEWELLAN FOREST PARK

It's all too pat,
too perfectly controlled:
first to greet the eye
great Roundhead oaks with rippled roots
that occupy the middle space
of rolling, English looking fold;
then the lake's unwrinkled face,
fringed by bright embroidered trees
and colour coded walks,
reflects
a showcase castle, pale and flat,
against a picture postcard sky;
an arboretum wall protects
well-bred exotic pedigrees
from roughneck native mountain breeze
and lowborn local shoots.
It's just too…. chocolate box;
one's almost glad of shitty boots
and stink of decomposing fox.

CAT

Intriguing things.
and not just to look at;
what jungle secret lies
behind
that blinkless blind,
the owl-stare green eyes
of a cat?
The gently throbbing motor purr,
the rippling wind-stroked cornfield fur,
soft-throated caterpillar curl
of a cat:
do these disguise
a sphinx-like scorn
for humankind
and beasts not feline born?
Dogs that are taught to beg
would come to mind.
And there's the playful torment then
of dizzy, dying mice,
mouth cuddling of the sentenced wren,
or the biting dead of a rat.

The answer lies
somewhere between
a spitting redmouthed fiend
and a whiskered rub against one's leg.

CHRISTMAS

The eye approves the festive scene,
the heart expands with Xmas joy,
the whole house packaged, neat and clean
as any gift-wrapped Taiwan toy.

Strung round the garden, fairy lights
irradiate the spindly trees;
the cherub in the holly might
well look vaguely ill at ease.
The coloured bulbs cast radiant hues
suggesting fairground's fevered glee,
the reds and greens and seasonal blues
reflected in the PVC.

Snow sprayed with taste on mullioned panes
evokes ye dayes of olde;
and safety-standard lanterns flame
to frighten spoilsport cold.
Inside the hall six angels bright
wield candles mains illuminated,
a yule log beckons from your right,
its fierce blaze finger regulated

The Xmas cards are neatly ranged
in drifts of polystyrene snow,
and plastic kisses are exchanged
beneath the plastic mistletoe.

The Xmas pud comes Ready Mixed,
there's sham champagne so "Here's Good Health, Sir",
and vacuum-packed, pre-cooked drumsticks,
and last year's crumbly Alka Seltzer.
Real wine comes from a cardboard box,
cigar smoke mingles with good cheer,
the spirit of Old Christmas walks
and hands out kit-brewed ginger beer.

Taped bells ring out the tidings glad,
a CD booms out carols jolly,
and even George, the inveterate cad,
admires the artificial holly.

It's sad for those out in the cold,
the mood is briefly sympathetic.
Roll on next Xmas, as of old,
Tra-dit-ional, no way synthetic.

CAUSEWAY WALK

I can't recall before or since
a walk so deep refreshing for us both,
one pre-set to condition saggy hope.
Someone had set the sea to Rinse
and tossed in scoops of soap.
The turning, churning waves and yellowed froth
untangled snags and sloshed away their fret.
It's biological, a wild walk wet,
something you should try,
to make dark musings white through cleansing kind.
Just set the feet to Start,
let the wind spin-dry
the secret weepings of the heart,
and still the tumble throbbings of the mind.

THE CHRISTMAS GROTTO BUILDER'S LAMENT

An object made is circumscribed
by the material fact
of its being.
One sees it all, and to the seeing
sharp filings of the steel-edged mind attract,
impelled by pull of critical gravitation.
But, hear a thing described
in words enchanting ear and inner eye,
and all at once sour censure's sweetly bribed,
and large imagination will supply
the wonder that the solid object lacked.
No craftsman's latex rubber flair
or painter's airbrush skill
can hope to please,
to equal verbal fabrication,
or win its instant facile praise.
A sample "fairy castle on a hill",
thrown off with practised careless ease
and gulped in by a willing ear,
defeats the builder's most exquisite care;
and, if a hundred hear the honeyed phrase,
a hundred splendid castles will appear,
each better than the one that's made,
all built on hollow sound foundation.
The one who builds on papier maché rock
can't tilt against the keep of lazy spoken charm.
Safe in the wizard tower of swollen talk
the fat tongue fears no harm.
The works of magic words will never fade.

CRITICAL MOMENT

"It's rough," he said,
tossing his landscape down,
carefully.
A pause for protest
(which, thank God, I did)
before he reassessed:
"I think at least I got the trees OK,
the yellow, orange and russet brown,
the mix of forest green and grey
and just that hint of red.
The wall's not bad;
notice how some stones have slid
and left a gap or two;
fairly realistic.
Do you like the way
the cottage windows catch the light,
the sunset shadows' length,
and touch of misty blue?
I'm glad
I got the tones just right.
Not that I'd claim to be
artistic
but doesn't the pond come over well?
Reflections are my strength,
somehow they make a scene complete;
the way it's done it's hard to tell
where trees and sky and water meet."

His scan had covered all –
a clever pond, soft rays, an honest wall;
nothing above, below, those careful trees
was rough, or failed to please.

DROSOPHILA

How, and why,
is there always a fly
floating dead in the vinegar shaker?
Is it comment on
the fate of man,
tossed and crossed by his sourgrapes Maker....
It's no use asking sodden flies,
they're in too deep for that;
I'll probably ask my wise-eyed cat
who never tells me any lies.

DEATH OF A FROG

Frogs can squeal.
Did you know that?
Yes, squeal, squeak, squawl,
you choose the word.
The stark fact is the sound;
not the puffings of the portly fellow
living comfortably in Toad Hall,
nor the warbled love strain
of one who did a-wooing go.
No,
what I heard,
and never would have found
but for that tearing, dreadful peal,
was the voice of pain.
There he hung on a wire fence
skewered clean through the side,
a helpless sprawl,
undignified,
absurd,
like some fat lady in a fall
with bloated bloomers of striped yellow.

Pawed at by my puzzled cat
the frog stretched wide
in literal agony of suspense.
Most odd of all,
something to be wondered at,
as its eyes filmed over and the creature died,
my heart could feel
the suffering of the Crucified.

DIVIDING LINE

Yes, the half ton,
fifty in a row;
and far enough for anyone
to have seen, to have been,
when nothing soothing salves corroded eyes
or lubricates a rusty mind,
and the engine fire won't burn
that used to light the coldest scene
like orange windows in a world of snow.
Pull down the blind:
no more station stops to go,
their nameplates' sudden smooth surprise.
This is not another junction,
it's a siding on the line of no return.
Thank God the memory still can function,
that it's able to recall
steaming horses in a stamping stable,
a drift of yellow roses on a farmhouse wall.

DOUBLE FAULT

I was born disadvantaged,
not having a fiery temper,
and handicapped
by eyes that saw another's point of view:
a double drawback
in the land of the loud,
where the mild-voiced many move in fear
and tiptoe round the rim of bubbling wrath.
I watched with wonder how from birth
some children found and used raw tantrum power,
slave mothers bringing offerings
to cap its red-veined heat.

Once learned, the tactic's never lost.
I see it every day –
unpunished infant swollen to adult threat,
his passage cleared of things that might provoke
a burst of uncontrolled, expedient rage.
Freed from the ties that bridle moderate men,
like patience, care for others, fair play rules,
the hothead glowers through his scarlet world,
and all the rest is sophistry.

DRUMKEERAGH FOREST AIR

Close your eyes:
you can listen better
without construing cloudshape skies
or tracing broken walls of stone
that ramble over hills.
The watchful ear hears branches groan,
the ear-shell oceanic sighs
of tall trees' windy tide;
a lost lamb's infant orphan cries,
drugged foxglove bees' ear-trumpet drone.
The stretched drum pings with highpitched flies,
and somewhere far away
a grey crow on the bare hillside
informs a pause with guttural caws,
scavenging for dead prey....

When days are darker, wetter,
and autumn leafchange chills,
rewind the mindtape, softly play
the mellowed music of a day
when summer never died.

EASY PICKINGS

Should you sit in
on a council coven raking through
the innards of some newborn scheme,
you'd find the time well spent;
or so it would seem
from an insider's point of view.
Once they begin,
this carrion crew,
intent
on scouring, devouring,
picking the matter clean,
they excise, incise,
conceptualise,
in a central heated argument
so needle fine,
they don't know where to draw the line.
(Or else they've nothing else to do...)
As cigar smoke and coffee steam
suffuse their work day mime,
poor purple fingers, never seen,
pour concrete for the thirteenth time.

ESCAPEE

Don't fret behind the bars of time;
unlock yourself, get clean away,
if only for one lazy, long,
emancipated, unregulated day.
There's nothing wrong
with adults wanting play.
For selfpity's sake don't try
that burn't out "I'm
far too bloody busy" alibi...

Head upon
a cradling lawn
soft furred as a peach,
allow the back to lie,
the eyes to partly close,
and squint up at the orange blur of the sky,
until your senses doze.
Listen to the green waves' lapping lullabye,
or swaying forest whispers, anodyne.
Lips faintly salt with spray,
breathing fresh with pine,
in conscience, can you say
these simple things are way beyond your reach -
the sweet surprise of everyday birdsong,
or cracking razor shells on a rum truffle beach.

FEBRUARY FRIEZE

It's probably no-one's favourite time of year,
but on a whitewashed mufflered day
I love that frostdust February haze
ice-powdering the silent air.
It's nothing like the curling autumn mist
that poets choose to praise,
but more a hanging sigh of winterbreath,
that nests in pencilled trees,
fringe-blurs faint spires in whitish grey,
and drapes a gauzy shroud on nature's bier.
You can't deny its chill of death,
as though a ghost has kissed
and drained land's life away;
and yet the foggy tissue veil
that rims the scene like iced-smoke frieze,
has cloudy wonder in its atmosphere
and all the distant magic of a fairy tale.

THE EXECUTIVES

The pattern was always the same:
someone, later unidentified,
unchallenged as to need,
would propose a ruinous change
for the others to "kick about".
Support came in from every side,
lame followers crawled into the lead,
and a gag was put on doubt.
Slyly a Parker slid your name
on a sub-committee to arrange
the tiresome workings-out.

The first defector showed with ominous speed;
for various reasons, all unspecified,
he found himself unable to throw his weight
behind the tottering infant scheme.
His secession signalled a rout
of all the major players on the team.
For some small fry the signal came too late.
Netted by self-esteem
they gaffed themselves like easy game,
deep-hooked as wriggling bait.
The happy uninvolved sat fortified,
and through strained sympathy would percolate
talk of promotion, their morning coffee theme.
While hunters argued who should take the blame,
mild snipers, old wounds sore inside,
eyebrows arched to draw a bead,
sure of their targets but nervous in their aim,
loosed small arms fire in sad anaemic hate.

All could have learned a lesson from my brother.
His point of view for me is now a creed;
the wise man is the one who doesn't bother.

FIELD STUDY

When the flock was moved to pastures new,
somehow in the hullabaaaloo,
one ewe was left behind;
a brambled, dowdy little creature,
it yet had one redeeming feature,
found most in human kind –
the need to seek companion, friend;
how else can lonely sorrow mend?
All hearts dread life alone,
but worse it is for sheep that need
to follow always others' lead,
with no aim of their own.

It chanced that in this same bare field,
beyond a spinney, well concealed,
there grazed a handsome mare.
With sheepish look, as well it might,
the ewe inquired left and right,
and found the chestnut there.
Who knows which made first overture,
and showed horse-sense, but this is sure,
their friendship quickly grew.
On daily walks, for interest's sake,
we'd call the mare, and in its wake
the sheep came trotting too.
Content it seemed to be a page,
an ovine extra on a stage
where horse-play stole the show.

That mare must know how Mary felt,
for where it cantered, galloped, knelt,
the lamb was sure to go.
Let others preach of poor sheep lost,
and ransomed home at priceless cost,
my tale I will relate:
the horse went back to Meadow Farm,
to stable straw and whinneys warm,
and soon forgot its mate.
This fond recital's woolly, twee,
not to be taken seriously,
perhaps it should be, though.
Go down that road, you'll hear the greeting,
a solitary ewe's thin bleating.
I heard it, just an hour ago.

FOLK CONCERT

Pale singer of the city night,
high priestess to the folk black mass,
down the sightlines of her voice
swirl echoes of a tribal past
peddled now in needy Dublin streets.
Soul-troubling child of fretful sleep
picked out in feverish spots of light,
who proffers fluttering thorngift choice –
ancient joy in sky-free lark,
or newborn heartwounds alley-deep,
soft watchfire songs against the inner dark.

GARDEN OF REMEMBRANCE

It was bad enough
that soft October morning
finding her lying there,
eyes gauzed, ears flat,
incontrovertibly dead.
Yes, bad enough
wondering if somehow
we'd missed a warning
the previous day
in the ungnawed bone,
the disregarded pat,
or back turned on an offered snack.
And wondering now
where
to dig the terrible hole,
and how
to tell the children down a phone.

I think all owners in their soul
have known this scene before,
right to the covering of a lovely head;
we hurl the thought away
like a random stick or rubber ball
that a dog keeps bringing back.

Worst of all,
unarguably real,
her daughter watching at the door
and the half wag of a hopeful tail.

HEART HEARD

You hear with pleasure how,
half-startled into an experimental trot,
a horse skims hoof thuds flat across the ground;
perhaps the sicksore lowing of a cow,
the tinny whingeing of a bearded goat,
or soft snout snufflings of a heavy sow
are what your heart holds dear.
Or is the electric squeaking of a bat
in velvet air the sound
your memory deepstores through the ear?
Some love, it would appear,
the measured mewings of an artful cat;
the harpy gull cries that surround
the worm-betraying plough;
a swallow rubbing marbles round and round;
the night fox barking cold and clear,
the throaty rook or grieving hound.

It's curious now,
with news, views, music, all around,
these sounds for me grow louder year by year.

HOMECOMING

And so it came about
that near the close of a hard November day
I found myself in wipered view
of distant Scrabo Tower;
almost home, at last.
Is there a better feeling -
warm tiredness motoring through the grey;
mizzle beam picking out
surprising neon berries, crimped grass;
smouldering beasts kneeling;
and only half an hour
from the one who
in all the earth
never doubts my present worth,
or fails to miss me, being away.

HEARTWORK

From early man's first sketchings in a cave
down to the print-outs of a modern age
our impulse is to draw the things we love.
With a graphic graphite care,
perhaps uncharacteristic,
we obey the need to put them on a page.
It seems that to behave
in such a marked designing way
is a labour self-imposed by heart's command.
Inspired by no prompting from Above,
having no creative flair,
and not at all artistic,
we stolidly portray
the object we are mindslaves of.

Back in our country primary school
red boys, pencil stubs in hand,
serfs in a feudal inner rule,
would form crude tractors down below
the long division sums and nine-times tables.
Girls would touch in pretty faces, wavy hair,
and ladies with outrageous hats,
or sometimes horses peeking out of stables.
Today those little girls draw fat pet cats,
dream-villas in a sunny palm tree land,
and plump blooms nurtured for the annual show.
No different is the case of full-grown men;
one I know,
for himself alone to see,
will reproduce, time and again,
painstaking likenesses of his LVT★.
I've seen a brute depict a perfect fish,
a thug exquisite coloured birds.
Perhaps our artwork makes a wish
far dearer than thick fingered words.

★ *Luxury Viewing Theatre*

HIDE AND SEEK

"Can you see me?" cries the child,
fists pressed hard against its eyes.
"Can you see me?" God cries too.
"I'm hidden in these scarlet skies,
in moonsplashed lakes of deep dark blue,
and dog-rose running wild.
You need to look in petal cups'
quicksilver drops of trembling dew;
at pink spots patched on rainbow trout,
the warm, wet licks of podgy pups,
if you want to seek me out.

And can you see through my disguise –
a Mayday cloak of fine-veined green,
the soft thick coat of winter white,
or golden braided harvest scene.
The wren's nest cuddles me from sight,
I'm curtained by shy morning mists;
the whispering caves where fog wraiths lurk
shade me in cool twilight."

More chance has child behind two fists
of being well concealed,
than He behind His handiwork
of resting unrevealed.

INVITATION

Come with me please
and listen to these,
the shiveringly beautiful harmonies
of doowop rock 'n' roll.
Now tell me, if you can,
that thinking modern man
since this scientific age began
doesn't have a soul.

HIGH RELIEF

Her miaowings pierced my heart,
the honey eyes wide with hunger,
reproachful,
finding me remiss, delinquent,
no cache of catfood in the house.
Too late now, the shops all shut;
no chance to buy back purrs of love
and sleek black rubbings round my feet.
Not so! A desperate cupboard rummage and,
like joyful manna from above,
a tin of tuna steak came down....

With peace restored,
I settled to a TV show.
No point in watching late night news –
black children swollen-bellied, thin,
mosquitoes stuck round wide dark eyes,
and wizened women mantis-limbed.
Across on lively Channel 4
I caught the stirring battle scenes
of an old war film, action packed,
in lovely black and white.

HUNTER-GATHERER

He presses pretty rhymes between crisp pages,
preserving fallfresh beauty from memory-mould decay.
He paperhinges thoughts as rare as nectar,
wallmounts word pictures in lyrical array;
he pins bright fragile truths and frames fresh phrases
in clear portfolio of abstract art display.
The poet is a collector.

He snares the whirling force of fancy's windblown crazes,
impounds its soaring freeflight in verse forms' tidy cages;
he sets a tender keepnet, a trim soft-fitting wrapper,
enmeshing struggling life in lines of patterned play;
imprisons panting feeling, the fugitive heart spectre,
and apprehends the future of the present's trembling day.
The poet is a trapper.

Inside the album of his mind, the sanctuary of his pen,
a burning vision glows that warms the souls of men.

HIGH SUMMER IN DOWN

The senses barely take it in,
those drumlins' fretwork field display,
their rumpled rows of sweet tossed hay,
and yellow blaze of scrambled whin.

Abandoned railway banks, bridge humps,
small farms, their byre roofs age-bent,
hedge honeysuckle's swooning scent,
and nibbling twin-eared rabbit clumps.

A pony snickers from the shade,
grasshoppers cycle in the heat,
fat corrugated lambs butt-bleat,
mart markings bright dyed on their suede.

Slight-shouldered swallows on a line,
switching cowtail swiping flies
in meadow clover's velvet guise,
gold buttercup and celandine.

Wild roses' soft pink perfume dew,
bold magpies' raucous carrion brawl,
and south, above a lichened grey stone wall,
the brooding Mournes in misty blue.

JOINT ACCOUNT

How can the will work when the knees are weak?
When aged tormentor witchpricks every joint
and wrings from fixed resolve limp-limbed submission.
Racked arms pulse-ache, worn ball and socket creak;
clear aim, sharp pinned, no longer sees the point,
hot irons inflame the flesh and cool desire's ambition;
With frame of mind hard pressed, the vital force veins leak;
intention knuckles under the tightening screw of pain.
mindplans are pinioned fast as mortised muscles strain,
the body's cramped abode quarters poor volition.

INVERSE PROPORTION

See handwriting on a page
crumpled on the public ground,
and, caught by curiosity, you want to read;
the same page in an office or a school
would lie an age
attracting not the slightest heed.
Or drop a coin in a busy street
and lo its value, bright and round,
reckoned on a landslide – rule,
has risen, fallen at your feet.
Imagine what you treat quite cool
were owned by others, foe or friend,
and cold possession boils to tender patronage.
Perhaps you're asked to lend
some thing you haven't made use of;
you'll find your credit taxed by private need.
In the hands of the buyer
the unwanted toy or tool,
when sold at what should be a pleasing cost,
is once again an object of desire.
Likewise an item lost
is prized more then than when it's found.
The dull bird huddled in the cage
gleams rich allure escaping far above.
More fuss attends a random fluke
than ever earned by steadfast love,
and one wrong note of sharp rebuke
will drown an orchestra of praise.
Dark hours of brooding brows are passed
dissecting some fool's careless empty phrase;
the present's superseded by the past.
What's worse,
the final rub of the perverse
that makes caprice complete,
the joy of triumph won't outlast
the shelf life of defeat.

IRRITATIONS

I can't say that they're strong enough
to justify a word like Hate,
but these are things, you may agree,
that never fail to irritate:
cold ashes in a cheerless grate,
ads cut out from my new Spectator,
milk bottles empty in the fridge,
damp washing on a radiator;
the phone that stops as you pick it up,
the man who waits and sounds wise after,
weak tea, sitcoms, a squeaky door,
false tears, and worse again, false laughter.
The relish of 'I told you so',
the one who can't admit he's wrong,
the Sunny Spells that soak you through,
choir short and sermon long;
no towel, power cuts, painting gloss,
a sore back from a floppy chair,
computer lingo, barking dogs,
and summer midges in your hair.
Bland cyclists riding three abreast,
a tractor when you're in a hurry,
lost keys, loud whispering, battery flat,
and tankers spraying fragrant slurry;
the paint brush left as hard as board,
the lid left unscrewed on a jar,
the cunning, punning tabloid press,
and no hot water for a shower;
soft handshakes, queues, a dripping tap,
the home-made kite that just won't fly,
cheeky children, lumpy porridge,
and those who start their poems off with I.

SCHEDULE

Tomorrow we'll walk the mountain paths
and let lake waters lap our toes;
we'll picnic down a country lane
beneath the sugared almond rose...

Right now ripe clients are on hold,
fat contracts hang in static air,
sharp bosses check promotion charts,
and nurses wait with coronary care.

JOY KILL

Something crouches deep,
a perverse shapeless blot,
in the black of the human brain.
On the clearest day,
when the heart is light and jolly,
it will visit you with instant gloom
and overcloud your mood.
It's nothing stronger than the faintest hint,
a spasm, of mindpain,
and yet it can
sap the life strength, dark tint
the brightness of the way.
You've felt this more than once in solitude,
but often in a pounding room
of bonhomie and riotous laughing folly,
a dark moodstain
will slyly seep
into the fabric of your play,
a debilitating sense of doom
that makes the scrotum creep.
Sometimes your memory will scan
back through the lightning flashes of the head,
and isolate a fault, a sombre sudden thought,
that caused a leak of melancholy.
More often than not
the something bleak
that briefly takes your breath away,
is softer than the breathings of reality.
A long dead poet might have said:
Intimations of mortality.

PATIO STING

A sleepy, undistinguished afternoon,
warm breeze nibbling lazy leaves,
sky a smoky duffel grey.
Compromised by middling wine
I'm headless in a cushioned curl
upon the patio lounger,
my mind purring with nothingness,
work worries hung behind the door,
the radio crooning undetermined tunes,
time a drowsy stretch from now till tea.

Strange that on such a mindless day
comes droning through the woolly air,
faintly lilac scented,
a stinging sharp, unseasonable thought –
Some day I'd give it all for this.

LIP SERVICE

As you may have inferred,
the service we supply
is totally free
to anyone in the public eye
for half a day or less:
those fresh in private tragedy,
or stunned by headline lottery success.

We offer, drained of feeling, thought,
the handy phrase, the multi-purpose word,
to cover sorrow, joy, the lot.
They're made for radio, the popular press,
an absolute boon
to dizzy victims of a violent crime
attacked by hungry mikes from ITV.
We don't employ dead No or Yes,
or lifeless words like *pleased or irritated;*
our menu serves up more exciting choice:
furious, anguised, over the moon,
sick as a parrot, devastated;
a play on words from time to time –
how did you feel when your house burned down?
Absolutely gutted.....

By the way,
don't worry if a thoughtful sound
that intimates your own free voice
slips out.
The editor will cut it.

It's good to spread kind empty words around.
You know, at the end of the day
isn't that what it's all about.

NEW YEAR RESOLUTION

Grave cows
with serious liquid eyes
ponder the incense offered hay,
their breath fog hanging in the cold.
We pass,
crunching the lacquered grass,
beneath the pink and turquoise skies
of a January day.
A pheasant aims its burnished head to scold,
indignant to be taken by surprise;
it's funny how the hen will sneak away
as if to apologise
for no display
of deep red, green, and autumn auburn gold.
We cross a road of sloe-black glass
etched in the starched earth
which frigid lies,
silver cold as foil.
A question wriggles in the mind:
how do men, for all their sweating toil,
expect green birth
from a bed of chilled and barren blue?
Yet iceground has its worth.
It's something to do,
or so I'm told,
with killing imperfections in the soil.
Death leaves it pure, refined.
It seems that sometimes Nature too
has to be cruel to be kind.

SAFEGUARD

Time, you're a sneak thief,
stealing my days away
from below my very eyes.
And oh the disbelief,
the numb surprise,
each time I find them gone,
and the looking in those most unhelpful places –
the memory vault of yesterday –
contemporaries' faces.

From now on
I'll guard against the grief;
I'll stand
among a younger crowd,
keeping one hand
in the pocket of my shroud.

NOT TOO BAD

Rough it Smoothly, read the ad
above a Satisfaction Guarantee.
Now there's how life should be led
if an arrangement could be made:
nothing happening too uncomfortably,
the blow of Fortune just a gentle slap,
the slings half-strength, the arrows not too keen;
even a bad break not too bad,
leaving a fairly easy red
and, if not the rub of the green,
at least the run of the nap;
a clause whereby the darkly sad
would be lightened a shade
to peace of mind dove grey,
with pain or rain not quite enough
to interrupt the play.
Yes, I'd like well balanced smooth and rough
on even-handed scales,
no bed of roses or of nails,
and the dream of a whitish Christmas.

PRACTICAL CRITICISM

"Words alone are certain good."
Yeats had it right.
What wonderful intuition,
or so we were told.
For him it was a fact
that passion grew cold,
that men would blindly fight,
and something terrible, or was it beautiful, was born
once words became subverted into act.
But wait a bit....
What good are words on their own?
Not wanting to be rude
or critically unkind,
you're talking on a disconnected phone,
you're building a paper wall,
or firing off blank ammunition
if words aren't action-backed.
I've changed my mind:
the man was talking shit
and writing corn.
Words are no bloody good at all.

PROPER NAMES

What's in a name? The poet chose
to answer through the emblem of a rose.
And true, its fragrance stays the same,
wholly independent of its name.
But what about the sound, for heaven's sake –
a different name could be a big mistake:
suppose this lovely flower were called a fug,
or young men sent a deep red, long-stemmed spug;
would skin be soft and gentle as a bong?
The ear alone will tell you something's wrong.
Such strong words have their usefulness, of course,
foul language plies their brutal, ripping force;
their fricatives and rough erupting plosives
burst from the lips, expectorant explosives.
No sane man, though, would take the chance
of whispering them to kindle slow romance;
the very thought is madness, quite absurd,
a lover's tongue seeks music in each word.
What writer looking for a panorama
to stage the passion of his sweeping drama,
would set his tale in forthright Ballybunion –
the name has all the glamour of an onion.
And bitter too some children straight from birth:
is there a happy Horace on the earth?
is Cuthbert ever introduced with ease
except to those who love a spiffing wheeze.
Teen idols came as Fury, Wilde or Steele,
fat agents adding pounds through sound appeal.
The screen will be threadbare, the boards well trodden,
the day the leading man's named Cecil Snodden.
Smooth planners know the proper names to choose:
Ferndale Manor, Holmdene Mews.
As yet there's no exclusive Creggan Court,
prestigious, luxury Tullycarnet Fort;
perhaps in time, when situations change,
solicitors will dwell in Bogside Grange.

REJECTION

No. I won't gape
at the refinement of civilisation.
You don't impress me
with your culture and sophistication,
and all that lofty talk of man's innate dignity,
his essential moral worth.
You see,
I know where you're from,
and, if you'd just sit and listen, I'm
prepared to prove it true....
You had a father, so did he,
your great grandfather had a dad and mom,
and they in turn had parents two,
and so it went, or else the generations couldn't be;
which means you had some distant past relation
alive at every moment in the history of our nation,
and far beyond, to life's dim dawn of time.
Who knows for certain what amoebic shape
your first forefather opened cold eyes to,
what primal form crept on the steaming earth
from the blank litter of dark pre-history.
So, I'm pleased to tell Miss Intellectual You,
by due process of lineal procreation
you happened here directly from an ape.

SNOWBOUND

Persuaded into whisperings by the hush
of winter-whitened wigwam trees,
lake waters noiseless, dark,
we trace a path of frosted slush
past huddled iceform effigies
and hill ridge frozen stark.

A soundless place
of snowshapes, ice and us...
Should life itself hard freeze
under this cold sky's blush
and we be fossilized in time and space,
what finer casts than these,
what better case –
ice mouldings in a forest park,
a red sky tinting snowy trees.

ROBIN

You're a cheeky chap, and no mistake,
for one not big.
There you sit with feet of thread
knotted round a twig
too thin to break,
wire legs outspread,
puffed chest and bloodsoaked bib;
that perky tilt of head,
beak sharp as a nib.
Nothing escapes your bright eye-bead,
its flicks of spite;
the short stab speed
of quickflit tail and darting flight.

Ask other birds –
they'll say your heart is hard,
frozen white
like a winter lakeside reed.
Maybe then it's right
that, in among the merry words,
you're painted on my Christmas card.

SEASIDE CONFERENCE

Outside mad winds were ranting at the wall,
black waves were smashing on the rocks.
The delegates at the one-day seminar,
with folders, files, name-badges and clipboards,
swarmed in the carpet comfort of the hall.
Close clustered in a hive of cosy talks
they hung in heated air like humming birds.
Bright blazers cloned and new buzz words
droned in the draught-free insulated room.
Between workshops and plenary call they'd take,
while somewhere from afar
the sea's wild voice would boom,
a well-deserved, timetabled coffee break.

A useful conference, pattern for many more,
something the annual report could proudly show.
The rogue wind still is panting at the door,
the dark sea slaps upon the rocks below.

ROCHESTER
October 1997

As children quilt hid,
landscaped by knees,
contoured by bone,
are lump seen, bump shown,
so this city, from the reservoir,
swells through leaf crust,
butts through a golden fleece
of autumn trees,
burnt yellow, amber, rust.

Below, quartered in a grid
of interwoven avenue and street
sleep clapboard houses, neat,
with grinning pumpkin frontispiece
ubiquitous, bizarre.

Time lapse, shift focus, enter
the Eastman House in stately stone:
museum of Photograph and Film,
icon of the Image Centre,
shrine to Kodak's roll of honour pilgrim.

View finders choose their fill
of Greek Revival architecture,
a living heritage adventure
set in the ruffled-shirt time sector,
lovingly preserved Corn Hill.

Dead centre, gravesite peace
on laundered crest, smooth slope.
What trim mortal hand or eye
has framed the fearless cemetery
(close by the tumbling Genesee)
of boldly named Mount Hope.

Above these earthbound things,
yet symbol of man's reach,
fan out four shells, a double pair
of skyline wings
that crown Times Square,
inspired by a Walker on the beach.
This emblem cannot fail
to uplift eye and heart;
so too a scampering squirrel tail
in pleasant Highland Park.

SIC TRANSEUNT RES MUNDI

Objects live and objects die,
as do man and beast,
by natural law.
They pass away,
or at least
they cease to be about.
Time seems to hide or scatter
things you or I
have certainly not thrown out;
nor have they been destroyed or lost;
they're just.... deceased.
Precious little things that matter,
not in cost,
but as echoes of yesterday;
for instance, a jigsaw.
You know the English cottage type
that used to eat up pressing hours –
tall gable chimneys, bow-window bowers,
perfect thatch, infuriating flowers –
pretty, yes, but nothing one would swipe,
borrow, swap, idly lift,
or offer as a last-gasp wedding gift;
where is it then? Where too
my valued records, comics, clothes;
that favourite jumper, airforce blue,
with the large-eyed Sussex spaniel
begging in handknit pose
upon my game expanse of chest;
no-one could put down so dear a mutt,
so close to one's heart, but
he's gone, perhaps to Fair-isle rest.
Gone too my cherished Rupert annual:
In spite of searches everywhere
We could not find that yellow-trousered bear,
All were agreed it was really rather weird –
Rupert and pals had simply disappeared.
And where have whole collections gone
of marbles, stamps or matchbox cars,
the bits and pieces one should fondly keep.
You can't blame famine, earthquakes, wars,
pollution or the atom bomb....
I think things just get old and go to sleep,
or, as they say,
pass on.

SIMPLICITY

If you were selling you'd
stress a thing was simple;
simple to use or simple to erect:
a teacher marks your storytelling Good
if it is simple;
not hard to follow, easy to correct.
Why, then, if we should
value the straightforward and direct,
do we regard the man of simple heart
as we would
something inferior,
poor and crude?
It should be very easy, I suspect,
to find somebody smart,
a complex person, who'd
resolve this complication;
someone profound, a man of intellect,
to give a simple explanation.

UNDERCOVER CHRISTMAS 1972

We met in The Welcome Inn,
the snug's soft leather,
warm fire, whisky, gin,
and easygoing blether,
and I was taken in
good company together
until, my cover paper thin,
we faced December weather....
icy I'm in a culvert, dead,
smiling she shot me through the head.

STILL LIFE

Honest was the one* who said
there's a silent life in every man,
a part
unintroduced to parents, friends or wife,
quite separate and independent of
empirical reality.
It's distant cousin to the heart,
unrelated to the head,
and not on speaking terms with actuality.

This secret life is pure romance,
not in the sense of human love
as in the world that's real,
but the finest vaguest yearning of the soul
for some impossible, intangible ideal.
Often dormant, almost dead,
it quivers into being quite by chance;
a sudden colour, snatch of song, or smell,
a half remembered instinct of the whole,
like the silver moonlight tinkling of a chapel bell,
will touch it into life.

An instantly forgotten dream
defies the memory, yet its mood stays on;
so do these phantom feelings seem
faint mistings from a deep familiar well.
A few men try to see clean through the haze,
and talk of wishful longings for what might have been,
dredge up a well-used textbook phrase –
sub-conscious, déja-vu, association of ideas.
Better by far it is to simply feel
these faint vibrations of a life unseen.

* *Irish Author – George Moore, 1852-1933*

THE THOUGHTLESS LOUD

These are the thoughtless loud.
Like bad smells from a sewer
that spread in summer heat,
they rise up everywhere,
eyes eloquent of lowlife breeding
offensive under blade-scraped hair.
So immature, so amateur,
immune to what becomes a man,
they walk their long-legged girls
on the outside of the street.
You see them always in a crowd,
perhaps around a steaming van –
the herd is feeding –
or swilling lager, unattested wine,
New Age litter at their feet.

For them what's new is best:
no sense of culture, no appreciation
of things passed down, the great, the fine,
in ignorance not even unimpressed.
With aerosols and brash guffaws
they celebrate the next sensation,
converse by tabloid headline inspiration;
our cherished Past to them's a Never Was.

Sometimes their ear-ring music swirls
across our weedless lawns,
and rumbles through our slippered worlds,
where folk hand round mild tea and scones,
and no-one hangs out undies on the line.

Perhaps it's best ignore them, make no fuss,
let them enjoy, we'll quietly endure.
Of one thing I am intellectually sure –
they never feel the need to think of us.

WALTER COLOURS

Black boots new printed on the frost-furred lane,
the reek of pipe smoke blue on evening air,
orange embers winking warmth through cobwebbed pane,
and amber kitten curled on shadowed chair.
Alone, unlonely, Walter lived serene
his days of cornflower blue and stooked straw gold,
sweet lilac, speckled eggs; like ivy green
he aged, without the grey of growing old.
I raised the latch half scenting khaki broth:
no collie scuffing at the barn-red door,
no tan stains on the wax white tablecloth,
no stove-lengths stacked on tiled brown flickering floor.
Yellow leaves gusting down like churning chaff,
FOR SALE his peeling epitaph.

WATERSHED

Suppose for a moment
you had to name the moment,
that monolithic, monumental moment,
when youth gave way to age:
would you try to fudge the concern
and snidely say
that ageing doesn't work that way,
it happens slowly, stage by stage.
Balderdash.
It's on you in a flash.
It lands the very instant when
the mind no longer wants to learn,
declines to turn another page.
Forget the myth of loitering decline,
there's no slow downhill train from now to then;
regard instead the club of youth –
chewing the gum of new ideas,
toeing every zigzag line,
kicking the tyres of the latest craze,
but open-minded, free
of cynic's catacomb decay
and wise man's Sunday-suited fears.
Where does this leave me?
I'll tell you an historic truth –
I haven't learned a thing in thirty years.

WEST END

They sure don't make 'em like they used to do:
everything's been herded into change
and branded for the worse;
not just the ambling story line
of once-feared marshall now a shaking drunk,
laconic stranger jest a passin' through,
some lonely sorrow back beyond the bend,
whose fast gun saves the lady's mortgaged mine
and, just before the big kiss at the end,
outdraws the hired killer at high noon
as frightened townsfolk shelter from the heat.

No, the very territory's shrunk,
the frontier's in retreat.
Don't laugh, it's true,
too true for forked tongue lies:
what's happened to the thundering range
that drummed with bison hooves and wardance moccasin feet;
the yellow wavy plains where settler wagon's speed
strobed wooden spokes that seemed in fast reverse,
vast buttes in monumental overview;
or desert hell with steer skulls crescent-sunk,
and solemn cacti tall against the moon;
a ghost town withered white below dark skies,
its dust storm spooking nervous tumbleweed,
one loose board flapping on the dead saloon;
the probing railroad poking past dry creeks
and rugged canyon's warsmoke crest.

As a red sun paints the sky behind far peaks
the western rides off in the dying west,
and leaves the legend lying in the street.

WETLANDS

Cycling down to wave-washed Island Reagh
we stopped beneath a Castle Espie pine.
Who could pass by that softsell sign –
the offer of a Downy Duckling Day.

It's true, a child's best seen, not heard;
enter that Percy Edwards world of beaks,
the hootings, honkings, tootings, squeaks,
you wouldn't wish it true of growing bird.

Stand on the bridge and broadcast crumbs;
pert teal and macho mallard vie,
they V to bread with daffy eye,
or synchronise chic coiffured bums.

How can these seabirds be so tame –
with barely half a quack and not a qualm
they guzzle outstretched food from tickling palm;
some wildfowl hardly justify the name.

And who first thought to call it bird of peace:
ignoring hackneyed one fell swoop, the dove
mounts serial grain attacks from trees above,
aggressive as the glutton greylag geese.

We watch from sly strategic hide,
like air raid shelters in the Blitz
or bunker gun-emplacement slits,
the first shy Brent upon the creeping tide.

In fleece flotilla, as promised early on,
a fleet of puffball ducklings bobs en route;
moorhens, widgeon, eider, whitecapped coot –
loose flotsam round majestic galleon swan....

With cycle clips replaced we went our way.
A place of wetland nests and woodland walks,
reed islands, feathery tufts and sparrowhawks,
rode on with us to wave-washed Island Reagh.

WINTERWALK

Don't believe the talk
about winter:

it's when your nose is wet
like a cow's
face skin-cold but warm inside,
and fat-gloved hands begin to sweat,
you're on a winter walk,
past charcoal boughs
down roads ice-glossed
with tyre patterns mud embossed
hard and deep.
Horses snort through nostrils wide
in fields of frost,
and heavy smoking wheezing sheep
look on with crusted brows.
A walking stick's the thing to keep
a steady rhythm in your pace,
and sober shoes to guide
you through
filtered air and cobwebbed lace.

It's true
that winter's not the time or place
to feel that beauties die;
look at the hedgerows' layered grace,
the distant mountains blue.
What words have you or I
with evening splendour in our face
to state the wonder of that molten sky.

UP AND UNDER

Ultimate urban architecture,
state of the art design,
twenty storeys of polaroid perfection
slicing the night sky,
floor upon floor
of high tech, open plan office space,
a pre-formed ultramodern structure
of computer analysed dimensions.

Inside,
brushed steel helical stairways
coil through
aluminium laminate doors
on thermal insulated polyvinyl,
each unit's microclimate cooled,
clad in hammered metal tiles
and linear ceramics,
with modular ceilings to ensure
integrity of acoustics.

Yes, twenty floors of complex, brilliant strategy,
crowned by the central atrium,
its lattice-shell roof glazing
and smart perimeter stacks
a joy of technical and visual achievement.

Miles below
thin fingers trade white packets in the dark,
someone kicks a coke can down the street,
and *Sharon luvs Suggsy OK.*

UNFILLED FULL

It's easy with your favourite food,
you simply need to eat and eat;
even a glutton knows
when he's replete.
Less filling is the fragrance of the rose
than can excite
those subtle cravings of a finer appetite.
Its silk pink lingerie so sweet
enchants the mind, invites the nose
to savour deep
until the senses swoon.
Like some coarse ravisher you would
tear apart the filmy underwear
and crush the tender naked heart
to satisfy the passion for its warm perfume.
You'd eat it if you could.

Then there's the intoxication of a tune.
It drugs the brain, enslaves the ear,
leaves heady longings incomplete;
you wish to drink, absorb, consume
the harmonies so soft, so quickly gone,
that wake an arching vain delight
to hear them on and on
in warm-eyed mists of tears.

The need's the same in part
when fondling rabbit, dog or cat.
Smooth stroking's not enough.
Snuzzle your face between the dear veined ears;
so strong's the affection you are victim of
it suffocates a feeble pat,
articulates in handling rough,
and wants to grip, to nip, to bite,
in dumb expression of devouring love.

You won't appease the hunger, truth to tell;
the taste of coffee can never match the smell.

NARROW WATER

What I best remember
is not the flaming redhot flash
burning air and scorching eyes
that crispbrown morning in September
clear and fresh;
it's not the sudden, shuddering blast
thumping the brain like a mallet blow;
the tantrum of the trees, the stench of burning flesh,
the rusty taste of spluttered blood.

No,
the thing I can't forget
is my own short laugh of sheer surprise
on looking down at something wet
and seeing both legs blown off at the thighs.....
One was found,
they said,
thirty yards away,
the other stuck fast in a field of mud,
both boots still polished bright, but spattered red,
eighteen lifeless bodies littered round.

Today
what scrapes the blister of my mind
until it oozes grief like sweat
is more than memory of that senseless slaughter:
it's the itch of limbs long left behind
one sunny early autumn day
at lovely Narrow Water.

THEN & NOW

CINEMA GOING

We met today in a shopping mall
but, watched by the watch as usual,
I hadn't time to say too much;
parting we made, with no idea how,
vague promises to "keep in touch".

I'm sitting wondering now
if he remembered me as the picturegoing pal
who, tantalised by Front of House display
of screaming girl and giant alien creature,
would mastermind the getaway
from lunch or French or history lecture,
to take in at The Ritz
a thrilling sci fi double feature.
With anxious pleasure four or five would meet,
conscious of lovely vulgar architecture,
where bold marquee threw shadow on the street
and curved stone steps led inward towards the show.
The choice was Back Stalls, Balcony or Pits,
and I remember, clear as yesterday,
the brief confusion of which way to go.

What other buildings have a smell so sweet –
stale carpet, warm dust, fusty cigarettes,
Art Deco wall lights' dim red seashell glow.
And oh the warm excitement in the gloom,
curved in the tip-up furry seat,
secure in the dark red velvet womb,
with lies allowed about tarty usherettes.
More startling than the terrors on the screen
was blinking from the darkness of the tomb
into the stabbing light of a working day.

They're all gone now, as if they'd never been,
their names in local history gazettes;
Majestic, Royal, Regal, Regent, Rex,
Apollo, Tivoli, Forum, Coliseum.
They leave behind a thought with power to vex:
are friendships too the stuff of a museum?

DIFFERENCES

We knew our city cousins by that backstreet smell
of oilslick hair, dark pawn shop suits,
and mildly fetid uncooked pastry skin.
In fear we mocked the different way they spoke,
the highcombed quiffs perched on cratered faces.
And it was strange to us they couldn't tell
the difference between a tame cow and a bull.
Our bodies reeked of ivy, fern and whin,
our clothes were steeped in Cherokee warsmoke.
What drew us close was the campfire of their things,
towny things, not known at public rudimentary school:
blue billiard chalk, skull and crossbone rings,
and crepe-soled shoes as thick as hobnailed boots.

To them, and us, the country then
was a thing still wild, a tract of trackless places
requiring doughty exploration.
Should cousins come today to try again
the unchecked rambling rush of vegetation,
they'd find
chiselled hedges spruce and neat
and, posed behind,
brickgroom houses clean in a country street.

FERRY LAND

A yellow moon, a black night,
two lovers in a mothy park;
far below, the perforated light
of a ferry dicing waters dark.

Our dear hearts' wish, as hand in hand
we watched it flicker from the bay,
transported us from common land
on board that ferry far away.

———————

A yellow moon, a black night,
two persons grey upon the deck;
do snuggling lovers from that height
still watch this sluggish watery trek?

Each heart's wish warm, both faces bland,
as seasoned travellers' are, afloat,
transported us to serious land,
and off this creeping vulgar boat.

Which thing, it seems, in any case,
is more to do with time than space.

MINDSET

Enid Blyton, I'll never forgive you.
Your Secret Seven and Famous Five,
the little liars,
filled in my colouring book of dreams
with smuggler coves, hidden treasure,
piping hot drinks, blazing log fires,
simple codes, adventure themes.

Today it's still my pleasure
to be the greatest fool alive
for the cordial phrase, the feelgood yarn,
the yellowed map of buried schemes.

Even though
I know
the coves are fouled with dog shit,
the drink's just tea, lukewarm,
that codes mean Inland Revenue
and log fires hiss and spit,
I'll never forswear you,
Enid Blyton.

ICONOCLASM

When first did truth break in
to violate our virgin joy;
or did its insidious shadow always lurk
at the edge of every dream?
We'd read with wonder how Rob Roy,
with tartan skirl and deadly dirk,
would lay his handsome hunted head
on bracken couch or dry cave floor,
betrayed in village, croft and kirk.

We built a ferny hut with secret door,
to thwart a Redcoat's musket lead
or wrecking rival boy.
There, in fugitive emulation
we stretched upon a heather bed....
In truth, did dashing heroes, or their kith and kin,
contend with earwig infestation
or the rancid reek of rotting vegetation?
No better was the cave we shaped to store
our nuts and weapons in ragged rabbit skin.
In spite of major insulation work
the dripping moss and green slime spread,
and mildew spawned in streaming condensation.

Why did the magic fail
and broken faiths begin;
did honesty demand we recognise the real?
Perhaps instead
there came the fatal vision of a pony tail
and a shy sleek slick of Saturday night Brylcreem.

THE LAND BEYOND FIFTY

The myths are dead
that nourished life and coloured youth.
It seems that overnight they died,
leaving a sterile world behind.
Rich lands of self-belief have dried
into a desert of doubt,
where confidence has fled
and flapping hope can never fly.
Streams of half-truth, untruth,
and downright lie,
that watered a complacent mind,
have shrivelled up unfed;
everywhere is drought.
Dread vultures of dead years wheel overhead,
prickly age-burrs spike the rough
and treacherous trail ahead
that peters out
below a rusty sky;
white bones of fact are scattered all about.
From under bleached rocks coiled death rattles quiver,
for countless miles the burning sands bake red.

But look, that desert is a bluff:
beyond there springs a sweet and gentle river;
the air is fresh, the breezes high,
the yellow grasses soft enough
to make the going kind.
No mirage, these are real
and safe from time;
at least that's how I feel.
These rolling plains are prime.
Off with the black tie.
Unless I'm blind
or common sense has atrophied,
I'm
as young and attractive as ever.

MOVING PICTURES

"You'll hardly know the place," said cousin Harry,
with laundered smile and nicely rationed nod,
my luggage large with thoughts he couldn't carry,
and points of view from twenty years abroad.

How right he was: it seemed a different country –
our village swollen to a throbbing town,
its ancient heart too small, the house fronts frumpy,
smart chalet forests growing all around.

But gone the tribe of dark yews caged by railing,
their flesh tattooed with arrowed heart affairs;
the Big House that presided through white paling,
its orchards hung with freckled yellow pears.

And someone's smeared a car park on the rye grass
where green apprentice drinkers sometimes lay;
the railway line's uplifted to a by-pass,
demoted narrow streets all go One Way.

And where's the Picture House that coloured vision,
suffusing dreams with love, adventure, war?
A planner's scalpel pen made swift incision,
and raised a bloodless supermarket scar.

An age of small shops selling buns and butter
has run out like the stopping of a clock,
their Roll of Service crumpled in the gutter,
the High Street one long type-faced office block.

The church stands still, blessed stonework tired and crumbling,
its roots time-fastened on the bone-marked hill.
At nights we'd hear the Faithful's musty mumbling,
and terrible women laughing in the Mill.

Why now do I expect familiar faces,
known voices whispering in an empty hall?
As long as memory breathes on precious places
the changing homescape hasn't changed at all.

ROOFED IN

When we were at the age of making huts,
mainly in user-friendly trees,
the roof was the all-important bit;
once it was on we would snugly sit
studying the maze of zipper cuts
that networked nettle-measled knees;
we'd sharpen hazel arrows for the kill,
and half hope for a kind downpour
that wouldn't show up doubtful roofing skill.
Such vagabond pride in being waterproof –
watching wetness through a leafy door,
rain beating on the suspect stopgap roof.

Neat slate tiling mutes the lashing
of slicing winter rain,
and in the roofspace woolly wadding
muffles guttergurgle splashing
and circulates warm air again.
Inside the foam-sealed, damp-proof cladding
of my velvet-curtained, cushioned room
I'm dry, securely settled, but.....
I think that I could leave this cuddling womb
to huddle in a leaky boy-built hut.

SMALL TOWN TRUMPET

I love small towns
that snooze behind white fences,
one eye half open should something choose to move.
There's no better place for growing up.

Seen from above ours was round,
held by hills in a wide-brimmed cup
but spilling over as a matter of course
to complicate the census.

We walked its worn streets' microgroove,
turned by the centripetal force
of slowtrack years' extended play:
ripe gossip dangling over garden gates;
seductive Picture House display;
sweet leafsmoke wafting from the cricket ground;
fumbling lipstick-flavoured dates;
beat music fizzing in the warm café;
a church bell from some distant higher source,
dissonant darker import in the sound.

I'd like to think some day they'd raise a plaque:
Best loved, unhurried small town of the year.
One velvet night in sneakers I'd slip back
and scrawl with civic flourish – *I wuz 'ere*

GOLDEN OLDIES

Forget arthritic knees,
receding hair,
and bop to the oldies' stomping beat:
as swirling dirndl fills the floor
awakened feelings flood the soul
through noise, smoke, perfumed heat.

Memory whirls to seaside summer:
welcomed back by annual signage,
Teas, Ices, Novelties, To The Beach,
it promenades past bristled sand dunes,
amusements, bandstands, yellow dresses,
loud jukebox rhythms in the street.

Oldies dig deep moods,
touch memories sweet.
Jive through the rainbows, the mischief of the music in you;
follow your feet.

THRESHING

That was the day,
the biggest of the year,
when the monstrous serious thresher would arrive.
We watched for it in joyous fear
and heard the cinders crunching in the lane.
Anxious wives and urgent men
paid homage to the power of the machine.
We too made sacrifice, all hope of play,
and joined in busy servitude,
warned rhythmically to keep away
from the tireless, slugging broadbelt drive.

To us the hulking wooden frame
was just the box that held alive
a beast
which gobbled up the pitchforked feast
and dribbled dusty grain.

Today
you'll find one glossy red
and clean
retired to the clinic of the folk museum.
In working vein

the thumping, shuddering creature swallowed stooks
in dullish pink with moments of orange lead.
Our task was watching sacks on hooks
fill up and bulge out hard.
A packing needle gave each sack two ears
and into mind there slipped vague tales of vats,
and millers' sons, kneebooted cats,
the house that Jack built, rats,
and, irresistibly, a little red hen.

For us the opportunity was there
to spy on neighbours off their guard;
from glistening heads, a thing most rare,
cloth caps were raised to wipe off sticky sweat.
Sniggering we'd make a bet
on who was bald and who had hair.
From high above the dwindling straw stackyard
dropped down the protests of badtempered rooks.

Throughout the pounding day, proudly subdued,
the women carried water, set down food;
the dogs too had their harvest when,
the bottom sheaves from each rick pulled aside,
a race of squealing rats was briefly seen
before a frantic, tearing genocide.

I still can smell that rare
sweet freshness brewed
of clover, buttercups and bright larksong,
of strawy, mealy air
in which gold chaffmotes danced daylong.

With sounds and sights and smells so clear,
the mystery
is this:
what lives fresh in head and eye and ear
is buried now in library books
and catalogued as history.

THE WALL

Take a right past Pinedene Rise,
through Willow Chase and Poplar Close,
their landscaped redbrick undergrowth,
white timbers circumflexed against blue skies.

In flouncy-knickered tinted shades
each home's exclusively the same,
distinguished by the chestnut of its name –
The Beeches, Oaks, The Elms or Glades.

Down through the brake from No.5
the ceremonial whiff of charcoal grill,
fine Doulton ladies sunny on a sill,
chalked hopscotch markings on the chevron drive.

And then......the Wall.
The Wall, and things beyond
that mutter of a poorer place and time;
coped with the grey of flinty years
it screens bedraggled garden plots
that once saw fruitful service in the war,
their compost now the refuse of The Wellfed State,
burnt eggshell acrid in the smudgy air.

The Wall.....
Ivy hugged, spuggy speckled,
it shutters cobwebbed cinder paths,
mean backyard stalls, dry-toilet squats,
drab flatfaced houses filed in rows,
and streetlamps from the dark pre-plastic age.
There too, like some recurrent rebel theme,
child hieroglyphics chalked upon
the pavements' fractured flags.

FOUR WEDDINGS AND A FUNERAL

ROCHESTER WEDDING

Nosing down through skimpy cloud
and dark October skies,
Toronto's twinkling circuit board below,
we scanned ahead to Andrea and Chris,
the broad bright welcome of their wedding day.
That they should meet and somehow know
uniqueness in a love among the crowd
has stirred no ripples of surprise;
the Finger Lakes point nature's channelled way.
All that has gone before flows into this.
You two light darkness with your heart's bright glow,
and melt cold distance with your downhome kiss.

THEIR MEETING MADE DECEMBER JUNE

Perhaps you'd ask this couple how they met,
what chance or change, what fancy, fate,
once led them to their first shy, tender date
in Glasgow West End wind and wet.
For instance, was it just a lucky break
that mutual friends should bring together
in a half remembered street in winter weather
this twosome, now about to take
each other's hand in marriage bond.
I like to think it more than chance,
their magic meeting of romance,
like something conjured up by fairy wand.
But instant love is such a tender plant
when boy meets girl and fears she may refuse;
shy introductions over, heart and tongue confused,
he softly prays, "Wish me one Grant."
For those who like a whiff of fluke,
Rachel was raised in England's Bingham town,
Philip named for the Binghams, County Down,
a portent from love's cabbalistic book.
The rest is history, as commentators say,
and here we meet in pleasant Aberfoyle.
Enough poor rhyming. Let's not spoil
the enchantment of a wondrous wedding day.

ALLOTMENT

How much credit can parents take
for lovely things they find
growing in their child:
loyalty, strength of will,
intellect, fairness of mind.
What difference do parents make?
It's truly hard to say;
some lovely things grow wild,
just for simple nature's sake:
warm primroses in a sunny space,
bright buttercups along the way,
cool bluebells near a shady place.

But still,
one likes to think he owns,
if only in an allotted sense,
some part in tilling the ground
before he gives away
his precious produce, Deborah Spence,
shortly Mrs Elliott Jones.
Here today
this plot is rich in lovely things:
friends, family, gathered round,
marriage vows, wedding rings,
green shoots sure to grow;
standard words but rooted true-
"I will, I do",
and my lightly watered "Cheerio."

SWEET SURRENDER

For these marauders,
rapacious, predatory,
no tartan glory
scrimmaging, skirmishing over borders,
ragged raids in flinty weather,
eyes red, rebellion raw,
untamed, untaxed by English law,
defiant in the heather......

The same cold stars look down,
three centuries on,
where wild men robbed and raped,
the borders now a rural town
by architects landscaped.
The same hot blood beats in the heart
of Carol in Glen Lyon;
inflamed by merchant-chosen wine
and mindful of the mutinous art
in every rebel scion,
will she decline
refuse to acquiesce,
raise arms against the foreign liege
and spurn his bold request?
As night birds skirl in mountain breeze
she yields to landlord on his knees
and, careful not to tack on 'please',
softly whispers, 'Yes'.

ENDINGS

Caught by the scruff of my own politeness,
too weak once more to walk away,
I bear, through fumes of aftershave,
the battering from this endless bore.
Puffed pigeon proud of his power of mind,
innocent of triteness,
he holds the floor;
a wink of gold watch marks another wave –
"It seems to me, in my opinion, I,
Take for example me, personally speaking, my...."
Meaning blurs, nerve ends grind.

What can a victim do or say;
hopeful of their random rightness
I loose the fitful nod, the aimless yes,
for every story ends with his success.

It's painful even now to tell
of one who talked upon me as a friend.
His story finally reached its routine end,
and I remember very well
not going to his funeral.